OPENING AND BALANCING OUR SACRAL CHAKRA.

Opening and Balancing Your Sacral Chakra.

Series "Opening and Balancing your Charka's "
By: Sherry Lee
Version 1.1 ~September 2022
Published by Sherry Lee at KDP
Copyright ©2022 by Sherry Lee. All rights reserved.

All information in this book has been carefully researched and checked for factual accuracy. However, the author and publisher make no warranty, express or implied, that the information contained herein is appropriate for every individual, situation, or purpose and assume no responsibility for errors or omissions.

The reader assumes the risk and full responsibility for all actions. The author will not be held responsible for any loss or damage, whether consequential, incidental, special, or otherwise, that may result from the information presented in this book.

All images are free for use or purchased from stock photo sites or royalty-free for commercial use. I have relied on my own observations as well as many different sources for this book, and I have done my best to check facts and give credit where it is due. In the event that any material is used without proper permission, please contact me so that the oversight can be corrected.

TABLE OF CONTENTS.

INTRODUCTION.

The New Age movement has significantly altered the world's view of the chakra system. Today, chakras are viewed as energy points along the spine, each of which governs a particular aspect of human existence.

The chakra system is regarded as a single entity, and a continuous stream of energy runs along the primary channel of energies (the spine) in response to life events. Each Chakra is allocated a specific color from the rainbow's spectrum that corresponds to distinct human emotions. The chakras are thought to resemble funnels and are hence also known as "energy whirlpools."

The lower chakras symbolize our human existence, while the upper chakras represent our spirituality; as one advance in his or her spiritual journey, energy flows from the root chakra (placed at the base of the spine down to the crown chakra (located at the top of the head). However, chakras can be interrupted, and this results in a troubled life. Therefore, taking care of each Chakra and maintaining a healthy, open chakra system is crucial.

The sacral Chakra is placed right below the navel in the sacral area and represents our sexuality and emotions. This Chakra is connected with how we present ourselves to others and how we adapt to our environment. It is also associated with originality.

The flow of energy in this area of the chakra system is analogous to the scientific concept of cohesive forces of attraction and chemical bonding, which is why this Chakra governs how we are drawn to others and how we form relationships with them.

This Chakra serves as the emotional nerve center. Noting that the female sexual organs are positioned on the sacral Chakra indicates that women have a more emotional conception of sexuality than men, whose sexual organs are located on the first

Chakra, also referred to as the physical or root Chakra.

The sacral Chakra is related to the tongue and hands, which are communication and creative areas. The sacral Chakra is formed throughout childhood and its development is determined by how freely we were allowed to express our emotions during that time. When this section of the chakra system develops effectively and is kept open and balanced, it enables us to be emotionally and sexually accessible to others and to express our emotions freely.

Orange is the color linked with this Chakra. Various gemstones are associated with each Chakra to keep them open and restore their balance when they get disrupted. The gemstones for the sacral Chakra are Carnelian Agate orange Calcite and Tiger's Eye. In this GUIDE, we'll explore effective techniques for opening and balancing this Chakra.

Read on to learn more.

CHAPTER 1: WHAT ARE CHAKRAS, HOW DO THEY AFFECT US, AND HOW CAN WE MAINTAIN THEIR BALANCE?

A field of energy called the aura surrounds our physical body. Chakras are spinning wheels in the aura that govern energy flow into the body. If any of these become blocked (inactive) or overly open (overactive), the energy flow is disrupted, affecting our overall health and well-being.

There are seven significant Chakras:

The root chakra - Located at the base of the spine. When it is balanced, we get a sense of power and safety. When out of balance, we may experience impatience or rage, and our behavior may become impulsive, violent, or manipulative.

Sacral Chakra - Located immediately below the navel, a balanced sacral chakra provides us with a sense of self-assurance, assertiveness, and joy. When out of balance, we may experience feelings of lethargy and inferiority, have low self-esteem, and become locked in negative thought patterns.

Solar Plexus Chakra - located just above the navel, the solar plexus chakra governs our capacity for empathy. When we are in harmony, we are organized and logical—when out of balance, we may be sluggish and overly emotional, often impacted by the emotions and concerns of others.

The heart chakra - Located directly above the heart. We are kind, generous, and sympathetic when we are in harmony. We have great self-esteem and are tolerant of others. When out of balance, we will feel disconnected from our emotions and find it difficult to express affection. We may develop feelings of envy, insecurity, and resistance to change.

The throat chakra - Located above the throat and is associated with the communication. When we are balanced, we can talk freely and are sensitive to what others say. When unbalanced, it may be difficult to articulate our emotions. It is possible for us to be unfaithful to people or to feel trapped in events or feelings.

Third Eye Chakra - situated in the center of the forehead; when this Chakra is in harmony, it enables us to be intuitive and wise. We may feel overpowered by the emotions of others. When out of balance, we may experience feelings of disorientation and fear and live in the past.

Crown Chakra - situated at the top of the head, the crown chakra is associated with our spiritual connection. When we are in a balanced state, we feel creative and sympathetic. When out of balance, we may become vain and too domineering of others. Our imagination may be "working overtime."

Many techniques balance the chakras and other components of the energy flow throughout the body.

1) An alternative therapist, such as a kinesiology practitioner, reiki healer, or energy worker, can analyze the energy flow in your body, including the chakras, and rectify any imbalances.

2) T'ai Chi and Yoga are beneficial kinds of exercise for maximizing the body's energy flow.

3) Since each Chakra responds to a unique vibration, gemstones, colors, and/or essential oils can be utilized to balance them. Certain stones, colors, and essential oils vibrate at the frequency required by particular chakras. Simply burn the right oil, set the gemstone on top of the Chakra, close your eyes and visualize the color streaming into the Chakra to use.

Place a stone on each of the seven chakras for the total balance.

The essential oils for the Root Chakra are hematite, red, chamomile, geranium, lemongrass, peppermint, and rosemary.

Red Jasper orange, Eucalyptus, Lavender, Patchouli, and Vetiver are Essential Oils for the Sacral Chakra.

Essential oils that are associated with the Solar Plexus Chakra are citrine, yellow, cinnamon, juniper berry, and peppermint.

Green Quartz, Green or Pink, Cypress, Geranium, Peppermint, and Ylang Ylang are essential oils for the Heart Chakra.

Blue Lace, Blue, Eucalyptus, Frankincense, Rose, and Sandalwood are Essential Oils for the Throat Chakra.

The essential oils for the Third Eye Chakra are amethyst, indigo, clary sage, lavender, petitgrain, and sandalwood.

Crown Chakra essential oils - Snow Quartz, Violet, Bergamot, Jasmine, Palmarosa, and Tea Tree.

CHAPTER 2: CHAKRAS AND CHAKRA BALANCING METHODS.

The objective of chakra balancing, also known as chakra awakening, is to balance the body's energy. Chakras are energy centers, beginning at the top of the head and descending the spine. Your energies exist and operate similarly to your physical body. When one part is damaged or blocked, it might harm your emotional health.

There are seven commonly acknowledged chakras.

The key to sustaining a healthy life is maintaining a balanced root chakra. The root chakra is positioned at the spine's base and colored red. It addresses survival concerns, including food, money, and basic comfort. When essential areas of your life appear out of whack, the root chakra is the place to begin healing.

The sacral chakra color is orange and placed in the lower belly. It focuses on sexual connections, pleasure, companionship, and personal well-being; its element is water.

The solar plexus chakra is situated in the upper belly and has a golden color. Its element is fire and relates to the physical and mental body's energetic state. A healthy solar plexus chakra offers the willpower, concentration, and self-assurance to accomplish your objectives.

The heart chakra is situated in the middle of the chest. It is green in color and composed of air. As your heart chakra opens, you can express gratitude and love without restriction. As it focuses on your relationship with all of mankind, many consider it the most significant of the main areas.

Fifth, the color of the throat chakra (placed in the throat) is brilliant blue. It governs language, sound, and communication. An open-throat chakra enables you to express your emotions and thoughts healthily.

Sixth: The third eye, one of the most well-known chakras, is located on the forehead between the eyes. Its color, indigo blue, is associated with intuition and the capacity to perceive beyond the tangible. This Chakra influences your inventiveness, sagacity, and decision-making skills directly.

A healthy head chakra heightens one's awareness of the divine intellect of the universe. The crown chakra is placed at the crown of the head. It is the creative center where you connect with your higher self; its color is violet.

Your chakras are interconnected, so the domino effect can be devastating when one of them becomes blocked. Consider your body similar to the computer's hardware; it is a machine that functions as long as it is maintained and has power (such as food, drink, etc.).

A computer cannot operate without the appropriate software. Your chakras operate like a computer's software, utilizing their energy for certain uses. Similar to a computer, your energy system can absorb harmful energies. Like a virus detecting program, chakra balancing purifies the system to prevent long-term damage.

There are various recommended chakra balancing techniques.

A hands-on approach is a conventional method for balancing the chakras. It needs a comprehensive grasp of the chakras' interrelationships. Hence it is frequently advised that you see an expert.

Emotional Freedom Technique (EFT) includes tapping key energy points on your body and chanting affirmations and resolutions.

Gemstones are often employed to cleanse and activate chakras. You set particular stones on each of them and recite special mantras known as seed sounds.

Meditation is the most straightforward and one of the most successful techniques. It entails achieving a physically calm condition while concentrating on a specific chakra.

Balanced chakras can facilitate a deeper emotional connection to truly satisfying goals.

CHAPTER 3: UNDERSTANDING THE SACRAL CHAKRA.

The sacral Chakra is placed right below the belly button, is related to creativity and sexuality, and governs our sexual and gastronomic appetites. When this area is in harmony, we are in touch with our emotions and receptive to receiving and giving pleasure.

This orange-colored Chakra is the second and is positioned below the belly button in the lower abdomen. The color orange is connected with life, endurance, inventiveness, excitement, and happiness. It represents energy, warmth, and the sun. However, orange is less intense or aggressive than red due to yellow.

Organs associated with this Chakra include the uterus, ovaries, testes, large intestine, prostate, and circulation. If you suffer from premenstrual tension, ovarian cysts, irritable bowel syndrome, endometriosis, low back pain, or pancreatic or testicular diseases, this is the Chakra you need to focus on.

It also represents self-acceptance, allowing ourselves to be who we truly are, self-respect, and respect for others. Self-acceptance is accepting and loving ourselves as we are now.

We may have things we wish to change, but as long as they are a part of us, we must learn to love and accept them. This is the core of our relationships and affects how well we can give and receive equally; it is the source of our life's passion.

This center is also responsible for duality. When opposites within us and our emotions balance, the relationship is healthy, and so are we. However, when there are extremes of either polarity, problems can arise. In its most extreme form, this is Bipolar disorder. When this center is out of balance, our thoughts and emotions can lead to depression, addiction, anorexia, or bulimia.

This one's Sanskrit name is Svadisthana, which translates to "holy house of the self." I adore this because we often forget that we are sacred and must honor ourselves, and this is where we do so.

This rotates clockwise in females and counterclockwise in males.

This energy center is about going with the flow, accepting things as they are, and simply existing in the present.

The color of this Chakra reminds me of sunrise and sunset when most people let go of everything and are simply "at the moment." It also represents hope for what the new day will bring or hope for the future.

This energy vortex is the source of our lyrical abilities.

Amber is the gemstone associated with this Chakra, so wearing or holding it while meditating will be beneficial. To balance this Chakra, focus on an orange image or a sunrise or sunset and repeat the affirmation, "I am creative, balanced, and living in the moment. I have healthy, loving relationships, and I am comfortable with my sexuality."

Then, direct your attention to your abdomen, to the "womb" region (or where the womb would be if you were a guy). Spend a moment observing the Chakra. Consider its color and vibrancy. Is it distinct, and is the color vibrant? The angel associated with this area is the Archangel Gabriel, who embodies purity. Therefore, allow her invisible hands to place any murkiness or discoloration in the area into a bucket.

She will cleanse your emotions of negativity and harmful addictions, letting you let go of relationships that have made you feel filthy. She will liberate you from your cravings for unhealthy food and discover that your thoughts and attachment to unhealthy food or excessive eating have vanished.

When she is finished, send the pail toward the sun's light to be purified. It is now clean, complete, and orange in color.

Attract orange creative energy to the space within and around you, and you will begin to experience a glow of orange. Feel the energy entering your Chakra and infusing it with vigor, clarity of thought, acceptance, and hope. Observe as it develops and spirals until it stretches many feet from your body.

The sacral Chakra governs sexual and reproductive organs, the spleen, and the urinary system. Imbalances in this Chakra can result in reproductive system diseases, menstrual or menopausal symptoms, sexual dysfunction, and a loss of appetite for sex, food, and, ultimately, life.

This Chakra is balanced when one is in touch with and able to express emotions, has appropriate boundaries, experiences pleasure, and moves with elegance.

Healing the imbalances linked with this Chakra involves developing a healthy relationship with one's emotions and sense of pleasure (in a healthy way.) Beneficial affirmations in this context relate to deserved pleasure, being in touch with and expressing emotions, and enjoying life.

The Emotional Freedom Technique (EFT) can be quite useful for identifying the emotional tone associated with an experience. I have repeatedly observed with clients how working with the Emotional Freedom Technique (EFT) on a problem while talking about it leads to identifying and releasing the underlying emotions.

Energy healing is also beneficial for similar reasons in a broader sense. Discussing an emotional issue during the intake process and receiving hands-on treatment can lead to recognizing and releasing feelings.

I have also seen that receiving energy healing and practicing the Emotional Freedom Technique (EFT), either alone or with a therapist, increases one's awareness of and ability to experience emotions completely.

Also, specific sorts of emotional healing can be beneficial. Inner child healing, previous life healing, and relational cord healing can release the energy linked with the initial harm, resulting in profound healing.

Tantra is a spiritual path that celebrates all aspects of life, including sexuality, as integral to spiritual life. As a result, it promotes a healthy, balanced view of sex and reclaims our right to pleasure (in life generally and in healthy sex life.) I believe that tantra and free dance techniques, such as five rhythms or biodanza, can be beneficial here.

Similarly, both biodanza and 5 rhythms dance foster emotional awareness and dance to different musical styles, alone and with partners. Lastly, the sacral Chakra's healthy, balanced color is a deep orange, and its healthy, balanced sound is "OH."

CHAPTER 4: SACRAL CHAKRA CHARACTERISTICS.

Consider the passage from the first to the seventh Chakra as stages toward God-realization, incorporating all chakra characteristics along the way.

By making decisions and gaining life lessons, we advance on our spiritual journey, sometimes regressing before advancing again. Still, once we transcend the lower chakra lifestyles, with their materialistic and selfish goals, and experience life through the higher chakras, growing ever more loving, we realize that our spiritual side has always been there, just waiting to be uncovered.

COMPOSITION OF THE SACRAL CHAKRA.

When the sacral Chakra is in harmony, you have clear thinking, intact emotions, and an active mind. This Chakra is influenced by how childhood emotions are expressed or repressed.br>

HEALTHY FUNCTIONS:

Physically able to accept one's sexuality.

MIND: cope well with anxiety; love self; self-confident; have a sense of belonging; good humor; extends warmth to others; compassionate; express desire for positive personal power in the form of material success; authority; ownership; control; able to survive on one's own, take risks with resilience to recover losses; able to survive on one's own, take risks with resilience to recover losses; able to survive on one's own, take risks with resilience to recover losses;

SPIRITUAL: at ease in the physical world; intuitive; clairsentient; adaptable to change

DYSFUNCTION: It is activated by difficulties with having positive feelings about oneself and others. You may not like yourself.

Reproductive system; genitals; large intestine; adrenals; lower back; pelvis; hip region; appendix; lower abdomen; kidneys; bladder; constipation; muscular cramps; lack of energy; allergies; circulatory system; sciatica; ob/gyn issues; prostate; spleen; weight loss; inhibitions

MENTAL: emotionally explosive; overly ambitious; manipulative; delusional; sees people as sex objects; dominating; grandiose delusions; panic attacks; victimized; shy; scared; lack of trust; overly sensitive; self-negating.

SPIRTUAL: consider one's spiritual convictions to be the sole path

Bring orange colors and water into your space; have fun; dance; be receptive to change.

The sacral Chakra (Svadhisthana) has six petals.

LOCATIONS: 1-2 inches below the belly button, lower back, and sexual organs.

PURPOSE: desire; continuance of the species; ethical center of the body; desires; creativity; attitude toward all of life; habit change; inner child's home; learning to cope with fear and survival; faith

Kidneys, mammary glands; ovaries; testicles; prostate; spleen are anatomical organs.

CHAKRA PERCEPTION: heat in the area of the lower abdomen/hara.

THE COLOR is orange.

ELEMENT: water.

ENERGY STATE: Liquid.

CENTRAL: emotive; receptive to feelings.

FORCE: Prana.

GEMS; Pearl orange coral, bloodstone, carnelian, and amber are examples of gems.

MEDITATION: reflect on a sensation of tranquil well-being.

MENTAL/EMOTIONS: emotional; tears; pleasure; suffering.

NATURE: physiologic.

PLANET: mars; moon.

PSYCHOLOGICAL PERFORMANCE: sexuality.

RELATIONSHIP: identifying moral relationships that fulfill bodily needs.

SACRAMENT: Communion.

SENSE: flavor, emotional pleasure, terror, and anger.

SYMBOL: a pyramid without its cap.

TONE/KEY: Ohhh tone; D key.

YOGA POSTURE: cobra.

CHAPTER 5: SACRAL CHAKRA - SEXUALITY AND CREATIVITY.

Swadhisthana means "sweetness" in Sanskrit. The Sacral Chakra is regarded as the seat of pleasure and taste in its most expansive sense, including food, clothing, music, design, and color. It is all about attraction and sexuality in particular (sexual identity and pleasure rather than the primal sexuality of the Root Chakra). Also, it is the seat of our emotions.

This Chakra is the most feminine of the seven. It has a deep connection to reproduction and is governed by the moon, which pulls the oceans and seas and the water within our bodies. This Chakra is generally characterized by physical fluidity and grace when it is balanced.

The Sacral Chakra is symbolized as a lotus with six orange petals encircling a white circle (representing water) and a light blue crescent moon. They rise and fall as though influenced by the moon's tides. It controls fluids in the body, emotions, and sexuality.

Our bodies are primarily composed of fluids. This Chakra is situated between the navel and genitalia in the lower belly. It controls your spleen, reproductive organs (testes and ovaries), kidneys and bladder, and bodily fluids, including blood, saliva, and seminal fluid. We are approximately 75% water, and water therapies are the most effective method for harmonizing this Chakra.

Poor sacral balancing is characterized by physical clumsiness or lack of coordination. As they come to terms with their emotions and sexuality, adolescent boys generally have an imbalanced Sacral Chakra.

In addition to being graceful, individuals with a balanced chakra are typically kind, open, and trustworthy, in touch with emotions and able to express them, eager to perceive the positive rather than the bad, and transform problems into challenges.

A chakra out of balance produces guilt, self-pity, manipulative behavior, and envy. If your Sacral Chakra is overly open, you may neglect your own needs and become so preoccupied with the needs of others that you feel like a martyr. Sexuality is at the core of this Chakra. Thus, sexual issues, jealousy, and obsession can arise if it is out of balance.

This Chakra is characterized by sexual awareness instead of primordial sexual urge. It controls our sexual identity, ability to form intimate relationships, and enjoyment of sexuality. When in harmony, it can provide us with tremendous sexual and emotional fulfillment.

When imbalanced, different issues might develop. If your Sacral Chakra is closed or obstructed, you may become obsessed with sex or your sexuality, excluding all others. You might view sex as a simply physical, hedonistic, emotionless experience.

At the opposite extreme, you may become impotent or frostbitten. A typical reason for a closed sacral chakra is sexual abuse. It is worth noting that the word sacral is derived from the same root as 'sacred.' Sex is not intended to be a trivial, meaningless activity, nor is it intended to generate guilt. Instead, openness and empathy it is a source of enormous joy and pleasure.

The sacral Chakra is the Chakra with the most feminine energy. It represents attraction, particularly sexuality, and serves as the emotional hub. It is governed by the moon, and so signifies fluidity and grace. The sacral Chakra is placed between the navel and genitalia in the lower belly. It governs the spleen, kidney, bladder, and reproductive organs.

Since this Chakra controls all bodily fluids and humans is approximately 75 percent water, water treatment is the most effective approach for balancing this Chakra.

As we mature and come to terms with our emotions and sexuality, this Chakra is typically out of balance. Those with a balanced sacral chakra are pleasant, graceful, open to new experiences, and constantly optimistic. A chakra out of balance leads to negative thoughts, dread, self-pity, and envy.

A balanced sacral chakra enhances your capacity to physically connect with your spouse in a state of purity, resulting in emotional and sexual fulfillment. However, when it is out of balance, many issues develop. You dismiss your partner and perceive them as a source of entertainment.

Occasionally, the situation becomes so dire that you begin sexually abusing your partner and view sex as a merely physical act devoid of feeling. The name "Sacra" is derived from the word "holy," which means "pure," and sex is not a trivial or meaningless occurrence.

Chakra cleansing is an excellent method for achieving a healthy lifestyle. When our chakras are clear and well-balanced, it influences our emotional, spiritual, and physical health. Once the Chakra has been opened and cleansed, it is crucial to ensure that it is closed, as it is vulnerable to harmful energies if kept open.

The Sacral Chakra is the sacral Chakra and is situated approximately 3 to 4 centimeters below the navel. It oscillates between orange and the note D. It contains the forces of imagination, lust, sexuality, and procreativity. It is the beginning of a connection with others.

You will be artistically expressive if your sacral area is in harmony, whether you are artistic, a wordsmith, or expressive in your day-to-day activities, such as childrearing, your career, etc. You will also be comfortable with your sexuality and expressive in a manner that respects others and garners your respect. If you dislike sex or are obsessed with it, your sacral Chakra may be out of balance.

Many traditional religions tend to attach a great deal of terror to sexuality. This fear has been passed down for decades, with society either embracing it or rejecting it at various points. The Sacral Chakra has been beaten up over time.

Certainly, in modern times we are becoming more linked to our sexuality as a form of self-expression and a profound expression of intimacy; nevertheless, we still have a long way to go, and many individuals still struggle to have a healthy, loving sexuality.

Creativity has also been stifled and occasionally forbidden (Consider the Dark Ages, during which all creative expression other than religious art was completely banned). Now that we understand creativity as all self-expression, the greater our confidence, the more we express ourselves in whatever we do. The following exercises will assist you in balancing your Sacral Chakra.

- Change your perspective on sexuality by reading Linda E. Savage's "Reclaiming Goddess Sexuality."
- Explore your sexuality, which may need treatment to resolve any associated difficulties.
- Explore your creative side by using mediums that thrill you, such as colors, words, and

music. Don't evaluate the outcome; simply enjoy the process of exploration.

- Consult with an Advanced Energy Technician to address the condition of your energy system and any damage to or impact on your Sacral Chakra.

Developing your connection to this Chakra can be enjoyable. Understanding yourself and what is working and what isn't in your life is empowering, especially because when you encounter anything that doesn't work, there are ways and means to deal with it. The result may be a much more fulfilling and loving life.

CHAPTER 6: SACRAL CHAKRA BALANCING: SIGNS AND ADVANTAGES.

The sacral Chakra is situated below the navel in the sacral region and represents our emotions and sexuality with others. This Chakra's energy flow resembles the cohesive forces of attraction that regulate chemical bonding. Consequently, the sacral Chakra is linked with our idea of attraction and the growth of our relationships with ourselves and others.

As the sacral Chakra is primarily responsible for the fluids in the body, notably the fluids of the lymphatic system and the synovial fluids of the joints, this is where we acquire flexibility and fluidity.

The color orange and the traditional symbol for the sacral Chakra, the crescent moon, signify our emotions and the relationships we develop with others. The moon reflects the sun's light, much as individuals often reflect and share one another's energy and experiences.

Our body's energy center is the chakra system, which maintains our general health. Even if only one Chakra becomes blocked or unbalanced, the entire chakra system will be affected. This emphasizes the significance of maintaining each Chakra's balance and openness. An open chakra contributes to a balanced life and a general sense of well-being.

When the sacral Chakra is not open, or the energy that flows from it is out of balance with the energy of the other chakras, a person may experience intense emotional outbursts and sexual obsession. A blocked sacral chakra can also result in a lack of creativity, separation from others, envy, guilt, oversensitivity, emotional dependence, and a limited understanding of personal boundaries and limits.

When our sacral Chakra is not kept open, we typically lose our ties to our family and friends and revert to keeping things to ourselves. Nevertheless, the sacral Chakra is also associated with our sense of self-worth; a significant imbalance and blockage of the sacral Chakra could lead to self-denial and self-deprivation of anything that makes us feel good.

In addition to persistent lower back pain, adrenal exhaustion, sexually transmitted illnesses, and infertility, an unbalanced sacral chakra manifests physically as lower back discomfort, sexually transmitted diseases, and infertility. In the worst-case scenario, a blocked sacral chakra can lead to eating disorders such as anorexia and even manic depression.

Certain yoga movements, color therapy, sound therapy, and energy healing, among others, can be used to keep the sacral Chakra open and in balance. One of the simplest methods to maintain the health of the sacral Chakra is to wear orange-colored clothing and have orange ornaments and décor at home and work.

Having a strong sense of bodily satisfaction, emotional fulfillment, and creative expression is one of the advantages of having an open sacral chakra. Having an open chakra facilitates open and trustworthy connections with our loved ones. It typically evokes a strong desire for life, love, sex, and delicious food.

CHAPTER 7: HOW TO ACHIEVE SACRAL CHAKRA BALANCE.

The sacral Chakra is predominantly found roughly two inches below the navel in the lower belly. Have you ever encountered a person who, for some reason, exudes warmth, friendliness, and an abnormal propensity for attachment?

Well, this is the well-known indicator of an excess sacral chakra imbalance. Other symptoms of an imbalance include timidity, hypersensitivity, sexuality troubles, trust concerns, and emotional instability.

This energy area determines an individual's emotional connection and relationships with others. Unquestionably, everyone will encounter sacral chakra imbalance at least once in their lifetime. To maintain your emotional and mental health, you need therefore learn how to strike a balance. Doing so can significantly improve one's overall health.

Similar to harmonizing other chakras, this energy point vibrates with a distinct color and tone. The calming color of this Chakra is orange. Imagine a bright, healing orange glow emanating from your entire lower belly, concentrating intently on your breath and letting go of all your worries. This assists in regulating your sacral Chakra, reducing tension or illness.

The second balancing option is to dance as if no one is looking at an outrageous level. This has been demonstrated to be one of the simplest and most effective balancing methods. You will purify and balance this energy center by dancing your hips off while reaping the benefits of physical activity.

There is always some physical stress and emotional weight in the hips, which is why many hip-opening yoga poses exist. The sacral Chakra is in direct relationship with the lower abdomen and hips.

Focusing on major hip-opening yoga postures can also significantly regulate this Chakra.

Even though there are many hip-opening yoga postures, it is practical to focus on a few postures and practice them every day until you achieve the required sacral chakra balance. This may require time and perseverance, but the conclusion will be extremely satisfying.

While hip-opening yoga positions can do an excellent job of balancing the Sacral Chakra, building muscle can produce even better outcomes. Maintaining physical fitness relieves unwanted physical and emotional tension, completely purifying this energy center.

Moreover, effective conditioning exercises prepare the physical and emotional self for meditation. The key to balancing the sacral Chakra is achieving harmony with the other chakras.

Considering that an imbalance in one Chakra often displays abnormalities in all other chakras, notably the sacral Chakra, upon thought due to a direct connection, those seeking higher emotional and physical well-being must consider chakra alignment. During meditation sessions, attempt to release all undesired bodily and mental stress from the chakras.

It is essential to release unwanted tension and embrace new, fascinating experiences. Learning and attempting to release emotional and mental baggage is also essential to regulating the sacral Chakra. Some exceptional psychics can look into your spiritual anatomy and assist you in finding troublesome energy centers and maintaining and balancing them.

There are many emotional situations in which we become entangled in life. If you are burdened by emotional baggage, it is time to release yourself from this stress. There can detect problematic regions in terms of imbalance in energy centers and what other chakras may be affected by the imbalance and offer chakra balancing sessions with coaching or help.

Maintaining a balanced sacral chakra will introduce you to a magnificent new emotional realm.

Sacral chakra cleansing and balancing will restore your enthusiasm for life, rejuvenate your ultimate life goals and help you achieve emotional harmony.

CHAPTER 8: THE SACRAL CHAKRA OR THE ABODE OF THE SELF.

Our sexuality, sensuality, emotion, creativity, and passion flow from the sacral Chakra; as you can imagine, it is a profoundly powerful and automatic place in our energy, as so much of our energy germinates in this Chakra.

The sacral Chakra, which is ruled by the element of water, governs all bodily fluids, the reproductive organs, and the pelvic cradle/hips. Specifically, the organs/glands/body components connected with this Chakra are:

- Reproductive system;

- All bodily fluid, including blood, urine, menstruation, and tears;

- Hips, sacrum, and low back;

- Kidneys.

When the sacral Chakra is fully balanced, our emotions flow freely like water, and we are both composed and vital. We are connected to our creativity and concentration when the lower chakras, specifically the root chakra and the sacral Chakra, are in harmony.

Among the symptoms of a deficit in the sacral Chakra are:

- Fear of contact;

- Opposition to change;

- Dissociation from One's Self.

- Among the symptoms of an excess or blockage in the sacral Chakra are:

- Sexual addiction or pleasure addiction.

- Inadequate limits or out-of-control behavior.

- Emotional outbursts or dramatic behavior that is unpredictable.

The sacral Chakra is related to the warmth of the color orange, the fruit orange, and all meals and liquids having a pleasant taste. "Svadhisthana" is related to the sense of taste, particularly to sweet items!

The sacral Chakra is strengthened and balanced through all forward bends, backbends (seated, standing, and prone), and squatting postures (prayer squat) in yoga practice.

In your yoga practice, you might choose to focus on the sacral Chakra if you so desire. The potential of this Chakra to cause disruption makes it all the more important to have support at hand. Unless you are under the care of a trained yoga therapist who specializes in chakra balancing, you should not do this on your own.

CHAPTER 9: INDICATORS THAT YOUR SACRAL CHAKRA NEEDS STRENGTHENING.

The Sacral Chakra is the second most susceptible to being blocked or severely weakened after the First Chakra. The Sacral Chakra is occasionally referred to as the Sacral Chakra. It is found along the spine around 2 inches below the navel. It deals with self-worth, creativity, relationships, pleasure, and sexuality and is impeded and undermined by self-criticism and guilt.

Five Indicators Your Sacral Chakra Is Weak.

1) You are tortured by remorse and unwilling or hesitant to forgive yourself for past transgressions. You are always comparing your worth to others and

tend to avoid the company of people you consider to be more deserving or qualified than you because their presence makes you feel even less deserving.

2) You have a weak sense of self-worth that is extremely reliant on the approval of others, particularly those you feel to have power or authority over you. Consequently, you often view yourself as a self-sacrificing martyr, putting the needs of others ahead of your own while harboring resentment and self-criticism.

3) You are easily offended, hurt, or angered by the words and behaviors of individuals you believe do not value you. You become defensive and tend to criticize those who behave differently than you believe they should.

4) You believe that you are perpetually in need of improvement. You believe that you must constantly develop yourself to be flawed and deserving of love from others and yourself.

5) You often or repeatedly encounter bodily symptoms: bowel issues, chronic lower back pain, urinary tract infections, or sexual appetite imbalances (hyper or hypo sexual).

There Are Five Ways To Strengthen Your Sacral Chakra.

1) Reflection: Read or reread the Biblical parable of the Prodigal Son (Luke 15:11-32). In the prodigal son parable, the younger son believes that he did not earn his worth via his acts, whereas the older son believes that he earned his worth through his activities. Regardless of your religious convictions, Jesus presented this fable to help you comprehend the reality of your inherent self-worth.

The sage father informs kids that their inherent value to him cannot be acquired or lost. This is true of everyone. Contemplate this until you feel, viscerally, that it's true for you. Whatever emotions surface, let them surface and flow; this is what is stopping your sacral Chakra.

2) Revise your notion of self-forgiveness to be more inclusive. Forgiveness is to abandon the notion that you deserve punishment for your actions. Yes, every action has repercussions, but these repercussions serve as teachers rather than condemning you as unworthy.

Stop believing that your mistakes make you unfit by punishing yourself for them. It is ineffective, unnecessary, and obstructs your sacral Chakra. Consider your current circumstances as your instructor and look for lessons to assist you in making better decisions.

3) Sing the word "move" while prolonging the "ooo" sound for as long as your breath allows. The word move contains the correct vowel sound and refers to the sacral Chakra. Consider going on an upward rather than remaining mired in remorse and self-criticism.

As you hold the "ooo" sound, focus on your Sacral Chakra (two inches below your belly button along your spine) and attempt to feel it vibrating and glowing orange, delivering life and health throughout your lower abdomen and all of its critical organs.

4) Chakra Breath: Perform the "Bellows" breathing technique. Extend your lower abdomen in all directions while quietly inhaling via your nostrils (or mouth if the nose is congested).

Rather than breathing, concentrate on expanding the space in your abdomen with your muscles and creating a natural vacuum that draws air in automatically. Hold your breath for a few counts, then contract your lower abdomen and utilize your core muscles to squeeze out every last bit of air, drawing your belly button toward your spine. Repeat as often as desired.

5) Yoga Asana: Start with your feet wider than shoulder-width apart and your toes pointed forward. Placing your hands on your hips, slowly rotate your hips in a clockwise direction to create as large a circle as possible around your centerline while maintaining your feet still.

Breathe normally while rotating for twenty to thirty seconds clockwise, followed by another twenty to thirty seconds in a counterclockwise direction. Imagine breaking up all the crustiness and stiffness that years of self-criticism have built up in your hips.

As self-criticism and guilt are shattered, and the orange glow of your sacral Chakra begins to radiate, you acquire freedom of movement in all directions, both physically and mentally, and spiritually.

CHAPTER 10: THE SACRAL CHAKRA AND YOUR HEALTH: FERTILITY, DESIRE, CREATIVITY AND YOUR HIPS.

Tightness or stiffness in a joint may be attributable to an energy blockage in the Chakra or power center that governs that joint. In this instance, your sacral Chakra is responsible. The sacral energy center, Svadhishthana, is one of the chakras most commonly affected by an energy block.

For example, tight hip and leg muscles, the tension is holding the energy back or, as the case may be, containing it. While you may attribute this tightness to some other physical stressor, I believe that by becoming aware of what happens in your body, you will begin to recognize patterns or habits that are quite possibly associated with your sacral or sexual Chakra.

In certain contexts, the word "sacral" can be substituted for "sexual," but I believe this energy center is much more. It is directly associated with the reproductive system, the name sexual chakra, and creativity, desire, relationships, and transformation.

How are your reproductive system, creativity, desire, and relationships? How adaptable are you to change?

As with other chakra power centers, an imbalance in this one can cause the body to send subtle or not-so-subtle signals to the brain.

Are you paying attention to what it says?

And if you are listening, what actions are you taking in response?

As discussed previously, an imbalance here can appear physiologically as infertility, bladder difficulties, allergies, internal power conflicts, and rigidity in the hips and muscles surrounding the hips. Interestingly, an imbalance in this area could also lead to obesity. I say this with some apprehension because I don't want you to believe that you are now at fault.

Let's retrace our steps.

What did I mean by mentioning internal power conflicts previously?

My objective was to provide a concrete representation of an abstract concept.

You can envision power battles as being between "good" and "evil," essentially a struggle to establish either domination or a balance between the two.

What if this power battle was more of a process of giving and receiving in balance?

Reproduction, a significant aspect of the sacral Chakra, is a delicate balance of giving and receiving between a man and a woman.

Why can't we relate the balance between giving and receiving to everything else this Chakra governs?

Obesity and overweight are the results of an imbalance between giving and receiving. You are consuming more calories than you're expending.

The same is true for your interpersonal interactions. Exists a balance between giving and receiving?

Is there any existence of harmony between your desires and your artistic expression?

Where do you express yourself freely, and where do you hold back?

In a similar vein, are you over-expressing yourself? Is there a point where indulgence becomes excessive?

This is a particularly intriguing chakra since it profoundly affects how we may all potentially spend our lives.

Then, how do we combine all of this into our road to improved health?

Or could we?

This delicate balance between giving and receiving is a major concern. You must choose between extremes of overindulgence, extravagance, flamboyance or fragility, tightness, and chronic holding back or withdrawal on the opposite end of the spectrum.

The great news is that it is seldom as black and white as you might believe. The worst news is that we are already so caught up in the urge to identify ourselves that our emotions are so linked with our conceptions of what is good and evil.

What, then, can we do?

If you find that you are blocked here, that you are emotionally holding yourself back, that you feel "tight" or constrained, then your only option is to determine the cause or causes.

Because this is potentially a long-term or long-standing issue, you should approach it tactfully.

My recommendations range from restorative yoga to massage. To all forms of artistic expression, including dance, sketching, and singing.

However, the most crucial stage is acceptance.

Recognize who you are, what you are, and your capabilities. This is where you will find true freedom and a stronger, more balanced sacral chakra.

CHAPTER 11; ACTIVATING THE SACRAL CHAKRA ENHANCES YOUR SEXUAL BEHAVIOR.

The sacral Chakra, or "Syadisthana," is the sacral Chakra and is directly connected to the ovaries, other sexual organs, and the reproductive cycle. A lotus represents it with six petals, and its associated color is orange.

This Chakra governs our sexual identity and our ability to form intimate bonds. If this Chakra is imbalanced or obstructed, your sexual behavior will be affected. Your failure to get emotional or sexual fulfillment can significantly impact your relationship.

Sometimes a person becomes so preoccupied with their sexuality that they begin to disregard their partner and view them as a means to obtain pleasure. Sexual abuse is the most frequent cause of a blocked sacral chakra, and if it is not managed promptly, it can develop into a more complicated scenario that disrupts the partnership.

If you are looking for techniques to open the sacral Chakra, the most typical practice is simply meditation. Find a spot in your home that is peaceful and free of distracting elements. Close your eyes and inhale deeply. When you achieve a quieter and relaxed state, keep your eyes closed and concentrate on your sacral Chakra, essentially using your inner eyes.

You will soon observe a light ray emanating. If you meditate daily at the same time and place, your body and mind will become accustomed to your surroundings and take less time to reach the final level.

Our energetic bodies facilitate our experience and expression. Understanding the chakras improves our understanding of ourselves. To live a healthy life, we must open each Chakra. Awareness brings us closer to ourselves and allows us to heal others and ourselves.

When our chakras are clear and well-balanced, it influences our emotional, spiritual, and physical health. Chakra cleansing is an excellent method for achieving a healthy lifestyle.

CHAPTER 12: SACRAL CHAKRA AND SENSUAL CREATIVITY.

Sacral Chakra is the second of our body's seven chakras. It is situated adjacent to the first Chakra, the Root Chakra, and is also known as the Spleen Chakra. It is referred to as "Swadhisthana" in Sanskrit, which means "sweetness."

The sacral Chakra is situated at or just behind the genital organs in the lower belly. It is the second stage by which energy ascends to the highest Chakra, the Crown Chakra. This Chakra primarily governs the individual's creative and sexual tendencies.

The Chakra is related to emotions, sentiments, moods of desire, imagination, and fantasies beneath these two main parts. When the Chakra is healthy and in a continuous state of rotation, it bestows us with an amazing sense of creativity. It also stimulates sexual cravings, enhancing our capacity for touch, connection, and making love and intimacy.

Sensuality's vibrations permeate the body, mind, and soul, allowing us to convey love to others and accept their love. When our creative impulses are aroused, fresh ideas explode. The difficulty of executing creative tasks that need a high level of inventiveness and out-of-the-box thinking is eliminated or reduced to zero.

Consequences of a blocked Sacral Chakra include the inability to establish positive relationships with others and to generate innovative ideas. Many circumstances result in the Chakra's obstruction or imbalance.

These include sexual or emotional abuse, chilly treatment, neglect, or rejection. All the actions responsible for the imbalance of the Sacral Chakra reveal a person's victim mentality. He may be emotionally burdened or wounded, impotent, aloof, have poor social skills, and suffer from stomach ailments. Creativity is lost, and movement becomes difficult.

The color orange is associated with the sacral Chakra. It is represented graphically as an orange pyramid surrounded by four petals. To restore the Chakra's balance, orange-colored things are extraordinarily advantageous.

According to some chakra specialists, one must have a happy and tranquil attitude to cure one's Chakra. For example, consuming a juicy orange, donning orange clothing or holding any orange-colored object. Its vivid vitality promotes the rhythm of the body's chakras. Since when we become restless, we prevent our Chakra from regenerating.

Sacral Chakra healing is crucial since it is this Chakra that permits us to live and work in peace. If we cannot connect with people via love and intimacy, our existence will be meaningless.

CHAPTER 13: OPENING AND BALANCING THE SACRAL CHAKRA.

The sacral Chakra is the Chakra with the most feminine energy. It represents attraction, particularly sexuality, and serves as the emotional hub. It is governed by the moon, and so signifies fluidity and grace. The sacral Chakra is placed between the navel and genitalia in the lower belly. It governs the spleen, kidney, bladder, and reproductive organs.

Since this Chakra controls all bodily fluids and humans is approximately 75 percent water, water treatment is the most effective approach for balancing this Chakra.

As we mature and come to terms with our emotions and sexuality, this Chakra is typically out of balance. Those with a balanced sacral chakra are friendly, graceful, open to new experiences, and constantly optimistic. A chakra out of balance leads to negative thoughts, dread, self-pity, and envy.

A balanced sacral chakra enhances your capacity to physically connect with your spouse in a state of purity, resulting in emotional and sexual fulfillment. However, when it is out of balance, many issues develop. You dismiss your partner and perceive them as a source of entertainment.

Occasionally, the situation becomes so dire that you begin sexually abusing your partner and view sex as a merely physical act devoid of feeling. The name "Sacra" is derived from the word "holy," which means "pure," and sex is not a trivial or meaningless occurrence.

Chakra cleansing is an excellent method for achieving a healthy lifestyle. Once the Chakra has been opened and cleansed, it is crucial to ensure that it is closed, as it is vulnerable to harmful energies if kept open. When our chakras are clear and well-balanced, it influences our emotional, spiritual and physical health.

The sacral Chakra is the Sacral orange or Svadhisthana Chakra. This Chakra is the sexual Chakra. It is located in the belly, slightly below the navel, together with the lower back and sexual organs. Water, emotional identity, and self-gratification constitute its direction. It is also related to our reproductive and sexual organs.

It corresponds to the hormone-producing testes or ovaries engaged in the reproductive cycle, causing extreme mood swings. When this Chakra is blocked, emotional issues and sexual guilt will undoubtedly arise.

The Sacral Chakra is related to the aspect of our consciousness associated with appetite, food, taste, and sexuality. In this sense, there is communication between our physical body and consciousness regarding the physical body's desires, requirements, and pleasures. It could be sex, food, or children.

The sacral Chakra involves a deeper examination of creativity, emotional connections, respecting relationships, letting go, dualism, magnetism, and managing patterns. Maintaining the balance and alignment of this Chakra is necessary to avoid experiencing physical problems.

Low back discomfort, decreased libido, sciatica, pelvic pain, and urinary issues are a few symptoms. The problem is discovering and assessing what motivates us to make or make the best decisions. We must reduce control issues, achieve balance and strive for a good yin-yang relationship.

We can initiate deliberate life adjustments by recognizing that acceptance and rejection are not the only relationship possibilities. This will guarantee a healthy sacral chakra. Then we will be certain to have enhanced creativity, increased emotional satisfaction, a great deal of physical energy, sexual vitality, a healthy self-image, and a zest for life.

CHAPTER 14: THE RELATIONSHIP BETWEEN CRYSTAL HEALING AND THE SACRAL CHAKRA.

Just below the naval is the Sacral or Naval (Belly) Chakra.

There are 6 petals.

- It regulates the reproductive organs.

- The gonads comprise the endocrine glands.

- It is connected to the Ethereal/Astral plane.

- This Chakra's color is orange.

- This Chakra's crystal is Orange Aventurine.

Below the navel and over the pubic bone is the Sacral Chakra. The obstructions of this Chakra are widespread in modern society. Here is where we discover the motivation to act on our desires.

Unless you had a nurturing and loving upbringing and were not impacted by the western world, it is nearly hard to acquire a balanced Sacral Chakra in modern times. The Sacral Chakra is the energy point that regulates your desires, sexual demands, and the amount of abundance you permit.

This Chakra is very feminine; when blocked, it manifests as problems with reproduction, feminine identity, aggression, sexual dysfunctions, apathy, back pain, urinary tract problems, lack of control over physical desires, and feelings of being creatively cut off; you may also become rigid and unemotional.

This Chakra is concerned with sexuality, creativity, and socialization. It is the site of happiness and the location of the inner kid. It is related to the testes and ovaries in men and women. Here is where the desire to procreate resides. Often, when people experience relationship troubles, this Chakra is out of balance.

When resolving issues involving sex, power, and money. Most people's lives are driven by sexual desire. Unfortunately, some manipulate others through sex to get what they want. Although the sacral Chakra is strongly associated with the misuse of sexual energies, its negative aspects are also associated with power and wealth. The sacral and solar plexus chakras are intimately connected.

The sacral chakra energy is transferred to the throat chakra. People use the power of language to manipulate to achieve their goals. Those with an inactive chakra do not communicate their feelings and wants.

The following disorders are connected with an imbalanced Sacral Chakra:

Sciatica.

Testicular Disease.

Mood Swings.

Lower Back Pain.

Menstrual Problems.

Muscle Spasms.

Ovarian Cysts.

Urinary Issues.

The energy of the Sacral Chakra can facilitate movement, growth, and transformation. Also regulated by this Chakra are emotional pleasures, especially intimacy. Such as self-respect, learning to give and receive, and engaging in creative pursuits. The Sacral Chakra is also associated with emotional swings, empathy, guilt, obsession, and manipulative personalities.

POSITIVES: Innovative - Emotionally Balanced - Independent - Happy - Relates Well to Others - Sociable

CONTROL ISSUES: Destructive, Despondent, Obsessive, Overdependent, and Withdrawn.

A healthy Sacral Chakra enables us to accept and resolve life's obstacles creatively, comprehend and integrate our sexuality appropriately, feel and express our emotions, and enjoy life's joys. When in a condition of balance, the appropriate color is Vibrant Orange.

CHAPTER 15: THE SACRAL CHAKRA YOGA ASANAS.

The sacral Chakra is linked with creativity, sexuality, the reproductive system, the kidneys, and the urinary bladder. Pose in yoga can be utilized to heighten sensation. Performing sacral Chakra poses creatively and focusing on the pelvic region can help to center energy in this Chakra.

Butterfly Baddha Konasana, Cow's Head Gomukhasana, and Goddess Deviasana are three hip-opening yoga poses.

Butterfly (Baddha Konasana)

I enjoy a deeper investigation while lying on my back with my legs and feet supported by a pillow or bolster and a light blanket draped over my body. Perform this position seated or lying down. The soles of the feet are close together, forming a diamond shape from the hips to the bent knees to the toes.

I return my attention to the pelvic region and continue imagining creatively. Take deliberate breaths. If this pose causes emotional anguish and you choose to remain in it, focus on the physical sensations.

Cow's head (Gomukhasana)

It has the opposite feeling of a butterfly. At the thighs, the legs are crossed together, not apart. If performed in a supine position, the knees can be brought near to the chest or pulled away toward the floor.

Try the posture while your legs are supported by a pillow or bolster. Find the location where the pose feels most natural and concentrate on the pelvic region for five minutes. To increase chest opening, you can wiggle to place one arm behind your back, and the other above or position the arms before the body. Arms and legs are repeated with the opposite leg at the top.

Goddess (Deviasana)

Which goddess will you choose? From Africa - Osun, Hathor? From India - Saraswati, Rakini? From Europe - Demeter, Aphrodite? Will you speak to or for a goddess? Do you feel more or less like a goddess if you move your arms and legs? How about moving the pelvic area itself? The focus is on the sacral Chakra.

Deeply explore sensations in the pelvic region, from the pubic bone to the sacrum, by refreshingly performing the first two poses on your back. Conclude with the standing pose, Goddess. This could be a nice way to start the day; at the end of the day, you could begin with Goddess and end with the restorative poses.

If you feel comfortable, close your eyes while you dive into the waters of the sacral Chakra through yoga poses.

CHAPTER 16: EMOTIONAL SUCCESS THROUGH SACRAL CHAKRA HEALING.

How would you define success? Some individuals have a nice home life. Others desire a rewarding career. Perhaps it is to live a carefree life without ties or concerns. Whatever your definition of success, some prerequisites will help you achieve it.

Obtaining fame and riches may appear alluring, but without a solid social foundation, your concept of "success" may fall short of guaranteeing satisfaction.

Social networking is the current craze. It is usual to be a member of multiple social networking sites that facilitate communication and connection. In some circumstances, building and maintaining a friend list can be quite difficult, but is everything based on numbers?

If you're looking for suggestions on how to live a balanced and happy life, you need to look no further than the mystical philosophies of the East. Seven energy centers in the body support emotional and physical health.

Chakras are energy centers that require continual and careful maintenance. Developing a mindful practice of the purest spiritual goals is required, but don't be put off if it seems too much like New Age nonsense.

A deeper look at the first four chakras reveals that they practically illustrate what many people would consider the path to a happy existence. If you familiarize yourself with their associations, you will find a map that will assist you in finding your way.

The first Chakra, for instance, serves as a reminder that everything is interconnected - consider what we now know about the impact of human actions on the ice caps and the ozone -. In contrast, the fourth Chakra is all about love and forgiveness.

Among these is the sacral Chakra, Svadisthana, also known as the Sacral Chakra. It is placed just below the navel and close to the genital organs. It contains the secrets of life and creation. It shouldn't come as a surprise that its message involves relationships, creation, ethics, and money.

It is the cornerstone to success in family life, the workplace, interpersonal connections, personal conduct, love, compassion, and forgiveness. It instructs us to respect one another. How could we possibly err if we just did this?

To work on the sacral Chakra, you must increase the Svadisthana energy in your life. Utilizing meditation and sound is a powerful method for achieving this. Each Chakra possesses a mantra that resonates with the cosmos. Utilizing it helps to eliminate obstructions and restore energy flow.

Meditation does not have to be difficult. Find a position of comfort and doze off! There is an abundance of excellent music available online that you can utilize to help you relax and helpful ideas on how to do so.

Once you feel relaxed, inhale deeply and sing the mantra Vam (pronounced "vom") in a steady, low voice as you exhale. Singing it will assist you in perceiving its tremendous resonance. There is no specific number of repetitions or time limit, though the average meditation session lasts about 20 minutes.

Initially, do it for as long as you feel comfortable but attempt to do it silently for at least five minutes. Upon completion, rest on your back and become aware of the energy flowing through your body. It should flow from the root at the base of your spine to the crown of your skull.

After this, you will better understand the sacral Chakra's strength. The healing of the sacral Chakra will alter your attention. If you can attain balance with this energy and begin to relate to the world mindfully, then excellent relationships, creativity, work, money and ethics will follow. The foundation of happiness that follows is the key to achieving the other desires in life.

CHAPTER 17: INSPIRATION AND THE SACRAL CHAKRA.

Getting into your imagination might sometimes feel like attempting to extract water from a rock. The good news is that there are strategies to stimulate creativity, one of which is balancing your sacral Chakra.

Chakra is the Sanskrit term for a revolving wheel; chakras are vortices of energy existing in the ethereal body and corresponding physical body places. There are seven primary chakras, and they operate as energy intake channels.

The sacral Chakra, also known as the spleen or navel chakra, is positioned around two inches below the navel in the lower belly. It governs self-worth,, sexuality, and creativity and is related to desire, pleasure, emotional balance, and the abundance you permit into your life to meet your desires.

If this Chakra operates properly, you will enjoy enhanced creativity, increased emotional pleasure and courage, sexual vigor, and a healthy sense of self-worth. However, if this Chakra is obstructed, sexual and creative frustration ensues.

You may have difficulty accessing your creative side or have amazingly inventive ideas but difficulties executing them. Physical manifestations of a blockage include lower back pain, sciatica, reproductive problems, decreased libido, and urinary issues.

Fortunately, there are many tools for balancing the chakras. I've provided a list of some of the correspondences for the sacral Chakra and instructions on how to utilize these tools to balance this Chakra and so increase your creativity.

COLOR: Orange:

Encircle yourself in orange. During meditation, envision orange around this Chakra. Wear it, consume it (ideally as food) or use it to decorate your studio or workspace.

MUSIC: sensuous, flowing music with passionate beats (think "Sexual Healing" by Marvin Gaye). Use your hips, dance. Gyrate, baby, gyrate!

Gemstones include carnelian orange jasper, fire opal, and moonstone. These stones can also be worn as jewelry.

Sandalwood, jasmine, ylang-ylang, clary sage, bergamot, and orange blossom are ESSENTIAL OILS.

Utilize an oil burner to combust various oils. In a bath, combine 10 drops or use them individually. (This is especially effective since water is the element governing the sacral Chakra.) When you need inspiration, place a few drops on a handkerchief and sniff it. You may create a massage oil using almond oil and a few drops of essential oil.

Now that you understand how to stimulate your creativity take a bath while eating a mango, don orange clothing and jewelry, and start hip-shaking to a nice beat.

CHAPTER 18: THE SACRAL CHAKRA AND SPIRITUAL LIFE COACHING.

The sacral Chakra is called the sacral or spleen Chakra. It is around two inches behind and below the belly button. It is shown as the Svadhistthana mandala in Sanskrit, which means "one's own space." Its element is water, and a fish represents it.

The sacral Chakra influences the lower belly, spleen, liver, bladder, kidneys, sexual organs, and fertility. Also, the sacral Chakra influences our emotional body, desires, sensuality, and sexual drive. It affects our ability to cooperate, negotiate, maintain an open mind, and disagree with people civilly.

If this Chakra is imbalanced, we will experience liver poisoning, kidney disease, bladder infections, infertility issues, and sexually transmitted diseases. Frostiness and impotence are prevalent. Due to our concern with pleasure and emotional escapism, we may become dependent on sex, food, drink, or narcotics. These addictions are reinforced by denial of unconscious emotional trauma.

When this Chakra is blocked, stubbornness, arrogance, cruelty, paranoia, envy, mistrust, and obsession may devour us.

Whereas the root chakra manages the ego, the sacral Chakra governs the ego's shadow; therefore, when it is out of balance, we will deny this hidden aspect of ourselves. It is normal for persons who need to balance this Chakra to project judgment, criticism, blame, and condemnation onto others. Secret addictions and desires must be dealt with.

When this Chakra is balanced, however, we tend to be receptive to life, opportunities, relationships, and whatever occurs in the present. We are present and willing to fully embrace whatever the universe brings us, regardless of how "terrible" it may initially appear. We do not reject, react or struggle against the lessons that life seeks to teach us. Because we are receptive to life, doors open for us, and everything we touch appears to be made of gold.

Consultation with a spiritual advisor might assist you in unblocking and balancing the sacral plexus chakra. Cinnamon, vanilla, carob, sweet paprika, sesame, and caraway seeds are spices for healing the sacral Chakra. Orange peel, rosehips, annatto seed, cloves, allspice, organic peppermint, and organic lemon grass are advised for herbal tea.

Gold, citrine, amber, golden topaz agate, chrysoprase, lithium, smoky quartz, turquoise, malachite, tiger's eye, and yellow calcite are crystals and jewels recommended for healing.

CHAPTER 19: OPEN THE SACRAL CHAKRA WITH STONE THERAPY AND DANCE.

Most of us know that our body has seven energy centers, or chakras, placed at different levels, each with a unique function. Each of these chakras is a transformer of the prana or universal vitality that runs through the endocrine gland at the base of the skull. If your lower chakras are cleansed and free of negative impressions, energy can flow freely back to your upper chakras, resulting in higher states of consciousness.

According to astrology, the sacral Chakra in the genital region of the body is governed by Jupiter, the planet representing human consciousness. It emphasizes creativity and sexuality difficulties.

If a person is raised in a conservative environment with insufficient freedom to express emotions, it is possible that other areas, including sexuality, passion, and creativity, are also affected. To activate the Sacral Chakra, we must improve our pelvic mobility.

Among the most effective methods is to do various pelvic dance techniques, such as those found in African dance styles. According to a small number of African dancers, the techniques are primarily designed to activate the body's chakras.

To open the sacral Chakra and all the other chakras, there is a second approach that is increasing in popularity, which involves using various color stones connected with each Chakra.

However, ensure that the stone is cleansed with water and mantras are spoken before wearing it, as it emits positive energy. Meditation must be a part of everyone's daily practice because it promotes mental tranquility and physical health, all of which contribute to a happy existence.

When our chakras are clear and well-balanced, it influences our emotional, spiritual, and physical health. Chakra cleansing is an excellent method for achieving a healthy lifestyle. Many online courses provide a step-by-step breakdown of chakras and instructions on How to Open Each Chakra. People who have actively used these potent approaches have achieved mental, bodily, and emotional balance.

CHAPTER 20: HOW CRYSTAL SINGING BOWLS HELP BALANCE THE SACRAL CHAKRA.

It is essential that the sacral Chakra, the sacral Chakra in the chakra energy system, remains balanced, unblocked, and healthy as it performs essential functions.

There are a plethora of ways to balance your chakras, but sound healing with crystal singing bowls is an especially simple and effective technique. By reading on, learn what the sacral Chakra performs and how it can be balanced through visualization, affirmations, and crystal singing bowls.

What Constitutes the Sacral Chakra?

Sexuality, creativity, emotional connection, intimacy, and desire govern the Sacral Chakra. The site of this Chakra is between the lower abdomen and the navel. It governs the lower back, the hips, the sexual organs, the kidneys, the stomach, the liver, and the adrenal glands. Any abnormalities in this energy center are believed to produce illness in these areas.

An imbalance can result in a lack of emotional awareness, inadequate boundaries, detachment from your sense of pleasure, and excessive resistance to change. Well-balanced, this Chakra produces a sense of emotional satisfaction in addition to a healthy sex drive, open creative expression, zest for life, and complete enjoyment of life's joys.

Meditation for Sacral Chakra Balancing Using Crystal Singing Bowl.

The sacral Chakra's related note is D, and its color is orange. This Chakra can be easily balanced with a simple meditation and your crystal singing bowl. As crystal singing bowls are set to a certain note, ensure that yours is tuned to the note D. Designate a particular time and location for your meditation.

Take a few deep breaths until you feel relaxed and centered.

When ready, strike the rim of the singing bowl three times with the striker and begin playing by circling the striker around the rim. As you play, envision yourself inhaling tranquility, happiness, vitality, and self-assurance.

Visualize yourself, releasing dread, self-doubt, and tension as you exhale. Imagine being liberated from any constraints that impede your connections, emotional lives, or creative expression. You may also repeat affirmations, either vocally or silently. The following affirmations pertain to the sacral Chakra:

- I appreciate my body and treat myself with dignity.
- I experience joy and prosperity with each breath I take.
- I welcome sensuality, tenderness, and pleasure into my life.
- I have control over my sexuality.

Continue with this procedure as long as you deem it essential. Stop when you are certain that the energy is flowing freely and openly. You can also meditate for a predetermined period and quit when the time is over. There is no wrong method to meditate and balance your chakras with music, so experiment until you find what works best for you.

CHAPTER 21: BRAINWAVE ENTRAINMENT TO ACTIVATE YOUR SACRAL CHAKRA.

Brainwave entrainment is a technologically established method for opening, balancing, and activating the Sacral Chakra through purposefully targeted sound frequencies.

The sacral Chakra embodies your magical, sensuous essence, where you see life in everything, engage in the eternal ecstasy of creation, and where you create. Through the sacral Chakra, we experience the profound emotions associated with our physical manifestation. This is where you experience both your masculinity and femininity.

This is the emotional, sexual, pleasurable, intuitive, creative, friendly, and nurturing Chakra. All these elements are flexible and constantly evolving. The continual change is simultaneously a source of joy and anguish.

And you fear change.

The sacral Chakra informs us that pleasure is impossible without change. We build and discover differences via change. Extreme differences produce polarities. Polarities create movement and attraction.

Life is characterized by and dependent on motion.

If The Sacral Chakra Is Not Working Correctly,

Open Too Much.

• Does not appreciate being touched.
• Excessively emotional, with weak boundaries, sexual addiction, and compulsive attachments.

• Emotionally volatile, overly ambitious, manipulative, entangled in illusions, and overindulgent.

• Considers a person's sexual objects

Not Open Enough.

• Coldness, impotence, rigidity, emotional numbness, and pleasure phobia.

• Shy, timid, paralyzed by fear, extremely sensitive, self-deprecating, weighed down by guilt, sexual energy-clinging, guilty about having sex, abused.

Here are a few questions you can ask yourself. If most of your answers are affirmative, your Sacral Chakra may be blocked or out of balance.

1. Do you suffer from low back pain?

2. Do you struggle with touch, whether someone touches you or you touch others?

3. Have issues with your kidneys, bladder, or fluid retention?

4. Did you experience distress or trauma between the ages of 3 to 5 and 8 when your consciousness began to develop?

5. Do you struggle with any aspect of your sexuality?

6. Are you emotionally steady, or do your emotions swing between extremes?

7. Do you attempt to conceal or manage your emotions?

8. Is the child within you still alive?

9. Can you think unconventionally?

10. Is your imagination constrained?

11. Are your sexual relationships mutual and respectful, with no restrictions such as impotence or frigidity?

12. Feeling distant from reality and having difficulty living in the present moment?

13. Nothing in your life seems simple?

14. Are you enraged by being a victim?

An emotional disturbance, such as a fight, a loss, or an accident, might cause a chakra to become blocked. Fear, anxiety, and stress are frequent causes of malfunctioning chakras. When obstructions gather in the field, the flow of energy through the Chakra is disrupted. Disease and emotional and mental illnesses in the physical body are ultimately caused by these barriers, which disrupt the Harmony in the field.

Brainwaves entrainment provides access to the particular frequency required to open and unblock the sacral Chakra.

When the sacral Chakra is healthy, open, and balanced, you experience vitality, enthusiasm, and sociability. It can elicit humor and compassion. You have a sense of inner health and well-being and are driven to create.

Clearing and balancing each Chakra will permit you to live your best life.

Utilize brainwave entrainment, a tool that can quickly access and sustain the frequency required to activate the chakras.

CONCLUSION.

According to its name, the sacral Chakra is situated in the sacrum region of the lower abdomen. In this post, we will examine the qualities of the sacral Chakra and what to do if it becomes unbalanced.

This is the second of the seven major chakras that extend from the head's crown to the spine's base. The sacral Chakra, also known by its traditional Sanskrit name 'Svadhisthana,' is an energy vortex located in the subtle body that plays a crucial function in preserving the mind-body complex in humans.

The sacral Chakra is related to the color orange and is represented by a lotus flower with six petals. It affects the reproductive and urinary systems, adrenal glands, and certain digestive processes. The sacral Chakra is associated with imagination, creativity, and sexuality on a cerebral and emotional level.

Instability in the sacral Chakra can appear as reproductive disorders, kidney and bladder problems, jealousy, and addictive behaviors.

As with the other chakras in the system, the sacral Chakra can be brought back into balance using different techniques, including crystals and meditation. While meditating, placing orange-colored gemstones such as carnelian, citrine, or orange aventurine in the lower abdomen may positively influence this Chakra.

Even if you choose not to utilize crystals, a meditation on its own can be quite effective, particularly if you use a brainwave entrainment meditation CD made specifically for rebalancing the Sacral Chakra.

If you are unfamiliar with brainwave meditation, it consists of listening to repeating sounds of precise frequencies. These sounds can directly affect the brain, making it simpler to attain various altered states.

In the case of chakra meditation, such a recording may also contain sounds corresponding to the frequencies associated with healthy chakra function (as with all other parts of the physical and energetic bodies, the chakras are vibrational and are thus susceptible to influence by other vibrational forces such as sound).

If you opt to employ a brainwave recording to balance the functioning of your chakras, be sure to set aside time daily to listen. As with any endeavor, achieving the best outcomes with repeated practice is more common. However, some people may achieve excellent results on their first attempt.

This book is part of an ongoing collection called "Opening and Balancing Your Chakra's"

1. Unblocking your 3rd Eye
2. Opening and Balancing your Heart Chakra
3. Opening and Balancing your Crown Chakra
4. Opening and Balancing your Throat Chakra
5. Opening and Balancing your Solar Plexu Chakra
6. Opening and Balancing your Sacral Chakra
7. Opening and Balancing your Root Chakra.

Other Series by Sherry Lee

"Why Alternative Medicine Works"

1. Why Yoga Works
2. Why Chakra Works
3. Why Massage Therapy Works
4. Why Reflexology Works
5. Why Acupuncture Works
6. Why Reiki Works
7. Why Meditation Works
8. Why Hypnosis Works
9. Why Colon Cleansing Works
10. Why NLP (Neuro Linguistic Programming) Works
11. Why Energy Healing Works
12. Why Foot Detoxing Works

13. Why Singing Bowls Works.

14. Why Tapping Works

15. Why Muscle Testing Works.

"Using Sage and Smudging"

1. Learning About Sage and Smudging
2. Sage and Smudging for Love
3. Sage and Smudging for Health and Healing
4. Sage and Smudging for Wealth and Abundance
5. Sage and Smudging for Spiritual Cleansing
6. Sage and Smudging for Negativity.

"Learning About Crystals"

1. Crystals for Love
2. Crystals for Health
3. Crystals for Wealth
4. Crystals for Spiritual Cleansing
5. Crystals for Removing Negativity.

"What Every Newlywed Should Know and Discuss Before Marriage."

1. Newlywed Communication on Money
2. Newlywed Communication on In-laws
3. Newlywed Communication about Children.
4. Newlywed Communication on Religion.
5. Newlywed Communication on Friends.
6. Newlywed Communication on Retirement.
7. Newlywed Communication on Sex.
8. Newlywed Communication on Boundaries.
9. Newlywed Communication on Roles and Responsibilities.

"Health is Wealth."

1. Health is Wealth
2. Positivity is Wealth
3. Emotions is Wealth.
4. Social Health is Wealth.
5. Happiness is Wealth.
6. Fitness is Wealth.
7. Meditating is Wealth.
8. Communication is Wealth.
9. Mental Health is Wealth.
10. Gratitude is Wealth.

"Personal Development Collection."

1. Manifesting for Beginners

2. Crystals for Beginners
3. How to Manifest More Money into your Life.
4. How to work from home more effectively.
5. How to Accomplish more in Less Time.
6. How to End Procrastination.
7. Learning to Praise and acknowledge your Accomplishments.
8. How to Become your Own Driving Force.
9. Creating a Confident Persona.
10. How to Meditate.
11. How to Set Affirmations.
12. How to Set and Achieve your Goals.
13. Achieving Your Fitness Goals.
14. Achieving Your Weight Loss Goals.
15. How to Create an Effective Vision Board.

Other Books By Sherry Lee:

- Repeating Angel Numbers.
- Most Popular Archangels.

Author Bio

Sherry Lee. Sherry enjoys reading personal development books, so she decided to write about something she is passionate about. More books will come in this collection, so follow her on Amazon for more books.

Thank you for your purchase of this book.

I honestly do appreciate it and appreciate you, my excellent customer.

God Bless You.

Sherry Lee.

Made in the USA
Monee, IL
19 October 2022

16204175R00066